THE GOD AND THE GOSPEL
OF RIGHTEOUSNESS

THE GOD AND
THE GOSPEL OF
RIGHTEOUSNESS

David Pawson

Terra Nova Publications

Published in Great Britain by
Terra Nova Publications International Ltd.
Orders and enquiries: PO Box 2400 Bradford on Avon BA15 2YN
Registered Office (not for trade): 21 St.Thomas Street, Bristol BS1 6JS

Cover design by Roger Judd

ISBN 978 1901949 59 9

Printed in Great Britain by
Creative Print and Design Group, Blaina

PREFACE

This book is based on a series of talks. Originating as it does from the spoken word, its style will be found by many readers to be somewhat different from my usual written style. It is hoped that this will not detract from the substance of the biblical teaching found here.

As always, I ask the reader to compare everything I say or write with what is written in the Bible and, if at any point a conflict is found, always to rely upon the clear teaching of Scripture.

David Pawson

Contents

PROLOGUE

Here is a really shocking story Jesus told.

Jesus spoke to them again in parables, saying: "The kingdom of heaven is like a king who prepared a wedding banquet for his son. He sent his servants to those who had been invited to the banquet to tell them to come, but they refused to come.

"Then he sent some more servants and said, 'Tell those who have been invited that I have prepared my dinner: My oxen and fattened cattle have been slaughtered, and everything is ready. Come to the wedding banquet.'

"But they paid no attention and went off — one

to his field, another to his business. The rest seized his servants, mistreated them and killed them. The king was enraged. He sent his army and destroyed those murderers and burned their city.

"Then he said to his servants, 'The wedding banquet is ready, but those I invited did not deserve to come. Go to the street corners and invite to the banquet anyone you find.' So the servants went out into the streets and gathered all the people they could find, both good and bad, and the wedding hall was filled with guests.

"But when the king came in to see the guests, he noticed a man there who was not wearing wedding clothes. 'Friend,' he asked, 'how did you get in here without wedding clothes?' The man was speechless.

"Then the king told the attendants, 'Tie him hand and foot, and throw him outside, into the darkness, where there will be weeping and gnashing of teeth.'

"For many are invited, but few are chosen."

Matthew 22:1–14 [NIV]

I am sure you realize that the king in the parable represents God, the son is his Son Jesus, and the wedding banquet is the marriage supper of the Lamb. The first shock is that the king kills those who would not come, and he burns their city. But the final shock is that because the invitation to the wedding represents preaching the gospel and inviting people to attend, someone who accepted the invitation and came to the wedding finished up in hell. For language like 'darkness' and 'weeping' and 'gnashing of teeth' is hellish language. Now I presume that you have accepted the gospel invitation, but this parable tells us that any of us could still finish up in hell if we do not bother to change. What a message! That is just an introduction, but bear that story in mind.

THE GOD OF RIGHTEOUSNESS

An opinion poll reported that 74% of the British people believe in God. That is a meaningless statistic because it was the wrong question to ask. The question which should have been asked first is, 'Which god do you believe in?' —because in Britain there are now thirty million gods believed in by the Hindus alone. Then there are Buddhists, who do not believe in any god at all, and there are Muslims who believe in a god called Allah. So they should have asked, '*Which* god do you believe in?' But even if the 74% said 'Well, the Christian God, the God of the church', you would still have had to ask another very important question: what *kind* of God do you believe in? That is the crucial question, and the answer to it affects your life profoundly.

At one stage in my ministry I was a chaplain in the Royal Air Force. There were three chaplains at each RAF station. One was 'C of E' (Church of England), one was 'RC' (Roman Catholic), and I was the 'OD', the 'odd bods' they called us, but it stood for 'other denominations'. When a hall full of new men arrived, what happened was that the C of E chaplain had first go, and he said, 'Everybody christened C of E come with me' — and about three quarters would go. Then the RC group left, and I was left with everyone else: Methodist, Baptist, Salvation Army, Presbyterian, Congregational, Buddhist, Hindu, Muslim, agnostic, atheist. So I was the chaplain to atheists, and I loved that job! When a man who was an atheist arrived, I said, 'Now sit down there, I want to talk to you. First, let me congratulate you on your faith. You have a bigger faith than I have. You believe that all this came into being by accident, by itself. That takes a huge faith. I don't have that much faith; I have to believe somebody put it there — much easier to believe.' Then I would say, 'If you die while you are in my care' (and many did, we were losing half our pilots every six months at that time), 'I will have the job of burying you, and I promise you I will not mention God. I will not pray, I will not read the Bible, and I will certainly not try singing a hymn. I will simply say, "This man is dead and gone."' And I made an interesting discovery: they do not mind living as atheists, but as for dying as one, that is a bit of a gamble! The third thing I said to them was this: 'Sit down there, and tell me what kind of god you don't believe in.' When they had finished I could always say, 'You have just made me an atheist, because I don't believe in that kind of God either.' Years ago, someone had said to me, 'Never condemn an atheist until you find out what kind of God he was told to believe in.' I found that to be very true.

What kind of God do *you* believe in? Even as a professing Christian, you still probably have many kinds of God believed in within your congregation, and it is vital to find out what kind of God *you* believe in, because you will need to talk to others about God sooner or later —and what kind of a God are you going to tell them about? That is the crucial question. Is he kind, or cruel? Is he good or bad? Does he care about us, or is he indifferent? These are the kinds of questions to which people want answers. What *kind* of God is God? And for the last hundred years the church has got into a habit of telling people that God is a loving God, and that is a habit that is going to be very hard to break. Break it we must, because I want to show you **that is not the way Jesus or the apostles talked about God to unbelievers.**

Now I have to establish such a surprising statement. It is a widely held view that the good news we have to tell the world is, 'God loves you', and I have heard many Christians trying to evangelise who are focussing on that statement. The affirmation 'God is a loving Father' is often added, and that is thought to be the good news that we have to tell the world. It came in just over a hundred years ago and we have been preaching it ever since, so much so that when I have shared this with some people, there have been those who have come to me in tears and said, 'I have no more gospel to preach now, you have destroyed my gospel.' Well what kind of gospel was it that it was so easily destroyed?

The last few decades have seen a twist in this gospel that God is loving, and it has come about by way of adjectives. We live in an age of adjectives which are constantly being used to exaggerate things. The Bible is very sparse in its use of adjectives. The Bible sticks to nouns; it sticks to facts, not fantasy. Therefore, you will never find the word 'fantastic' in your Bible — though you hear it everywhere else today. Does it surprise you to hear that you will never find the expression 'amazing grace' in the Bible? The modern equivalent of that is extreme — 'outrageous grace', but you will not find 'outrageous grace' in your Bible either. The adjective that came in some years ago to qualify the love of God is 'unconditional' — the 'unconditional love' of God. Did you find that word 'unconditional' in your Bible? It has become so popular that it is being used everywhere by preachers and by evangelists, but the Bible never talks about God's love like that.

What does that phrase 'unconditional love' mean

to the unbeliever? It communicates to him or her that God does not judge us, and will never judge us. We must face the fact that a 'God' of 'unconditional love' would never send anybody to hell, and yet Jesus himself said that God would do so.

We have a problem here. When you begin by telling people about the love of God they will immediately object. The objection will begin, 'How can a loving God . . . ?' and that will be completed in one of two ways. The first will be that they will point to the suffering in this world and say, 'How can a loving God allow all the suffering in this world, from tsunamis and earthquakes to cancer and AIDS? How can a loving God allow so much pain in this life?' That is the immediate objection you will get when you tell an unbeliever that God is loving. It is an obvious objection because it means that either God is unable to stop the suffering or unwilling to stop it, but he could, and that begins a criticism of God, a complaint about the way he runs the world. It implies: if I were God I could do a better job than he is doing, because I would not allow it.

The second objection is about suffering in the next world. How can a loving God send anyone to hell? I wrote a book on hell, entitled *The Road to Hell*, and it was a difficult book to write. In fact, the manuscript was lost in an Italian airport – the only manuscript, and I had hand-written it, as I do all my books. I said, 'Lord, what a wonderful opportunity for me to find out if you want this book published, because it is lost, it is gone, it has been stolen.' And I said, 'If you don't want it published, don't bring that manuscript back, but if you do, you know what to do.' The next morning, one hundred miles away, a man walked up to me in the middle of a street and gave me my briefcase back with all the manuscript in it. That is how it was published. It was advertised in a national magazine: 'Read David Pawson's autobiography, *The Road To Hell*'!

But after I had written that book (because of my deep burden that preachers were no longer preaching on hell, which seemed to indicate that they no longer took it seriously), I was invited to broadcast after broadcast for the BBC. Apparently it is strange to find a preacher who still believes in hell, and I was interviewed repeatedly by the media. The first question was always the same and it became quite boring: 'How can a loving God send anyone to hell?' I usually replied to that question with another question – I learned that technique from Jesus – and my question was, 'Where did you get the idea that God is loving?'

That really threw the presenter. The interview would continue something like this: he would stutter and stammer and say, 'Well, don't Christians believe that?'

'Well, as a matter of fact they do.'

'And didn't Jesus teach that?'

'Well, as a matter of fact he did, but everything I know about hell I learned from Jesus. Nobody else in the Bible talked about it. Paul doesn't, Peter doesn't, John doesn't, Isaiah doesn't, Jeremiah doesn't. Only Jesus dared to tell us what hell was like, and incidentally all but two of his warnings about hell were delivered to born again believers. The two exceptions were the Pharisees.'

What we have done in focussing on the love of God is to give people a sentimental rather than a scriptural understanding of God — that *he* is somehow there to serve *us*; we are not here to serve him; he is there to keep us healthy, to keep us safe, and to keep us prosperous, or as prosperous as we need to be; to keep us, in a word, *happy*. 'And if God doesn't keep me happy, safe and healthy, I'll call it quits with him and I'll stop going to church'!

I have met so many thousands of people who in effect are saying, 'He is no use to me, so why bother?' This applies to the majority of our fellow countrymen. Why aren't they in church? They will tell you, if they are honest, they don't think God is of any use to them, so why should they spend any time or money on him? That flows from a sentimental view of God. If he fails to look after us we complain, we grumble, we criticise. But if that is what God is like, I am finished.

So this raises the question: should we really be talking about God's love to the world? My answer to that question must be based on the Bible. I am a Scripture man, and I go to God's word for the answer to every question. So I want to draw your attention to one or two facts and, I beg you, please check me out in your Bible for yourself — that is my safety. I am not trying to share my opinions, I am drawing your attention to God's word.

Here is the first fact, and it is a surprising fact to many people: there is very little about God's love in your Bible. Direct references to God's love are few and far between. Less than one verse in a thousand mentions God's love. Yet to hear some preachers and evangelists you would think the whole Bible is about nothing else. But it is astonishing. Here are some facts: Genesis has not a mention of God's love; Exodus, one verse; Leviticus, not a mention; Numbers, not a mention; in Deuteronomy, one verse; in Joshua, not a mention; Judges, not a mention; Ruth, not a mention; 1 and 2 Samuel, not a mention; 1 and 2 Kings, not a mention; 1 and 2 Chronicles, not a mention. Have you ever realized this? If you only hear people quote the few verses about God's love, then you may think the whole Bible is about it, but it is not. There are one or two psalms, there is nothing in Proverbs, Song of Songs —no, not a word; Ecclesiastes, no. Come to the prophets:

there is one verse in Isaiah, one verse in Jeremiah, one verse in Ezekiel; nothing in Daniel; in Hosea, a few verses; Amos, nothing; and so on through all the minor prophets, not a word.

'Ah,' people say, 'but we are New Testament Christians, we live in the New Testament and the New Testament is FULL of the love of God.' No, it is not! There is not a word in Matthew, nor in Mark, nor in Luke. There are a few verses in John and, most significantly, not a single mention in the book of Acts — and Acts shows us how the early church evangelised. It is what they preached, it is how they went out and spread the church. You would have thought that book would be packed with the love of God, and there is not a mention. Why didn't they preach it? And yet that is what we go out and preach, and we think we are repeating what they did! That book of Acts raises the question really sharply for me: well, what did they say about God if they did not mention his love? And how did the church spread everywhere and grow? Whereas the churches in this country are dying, for the most part. Let us face facts. The Church of England is reported to have been losing a thousand souls a week; people are voting with their feet. Methodists have closed two chapels a week, and we are told that the Muslims are opening two mosques a week. Wake up and realise what is happening! We must not live in illusions. How did they do it in the book of Acts? How did the apostles do it without ever mentioning the love of God? Could you go out and evangelise without mentioning the love of God? We have so got into this habit that many Christians say they just could not do it. Well, that is the first big surprise, how little there is about the love of God in your Bible: one verse in a thousand.

The second fact is even more astonishing, and again I invite you to check me out in your Bible and, I repeat this, do not believe anything I am writing without opening your own Bible. **Every mention of the love of God that you find in the Bible is directed either to God in praise or to believers in fellowship. Not a single verse about the love of God is directed to unbelievers.**

Check me out! I put the love of God in the category of 'pearls', and Jesus said, *'Do not throw your pearls to pigs. If you do, they may trample them under their feet, and then turn and tear you to pieces.'* [NIV] As soon as you say 'God is love', they say, 'How can a loving God allow suffering in this world or the next?' There is an immediate objection and they turn and rend you.

Let us now ask about one well-known text. I own a book entitled *The Gospel in Many Tongues*. (It has 847 of them!) It refers to the verse John 3:16. Well then, what about John 3:16? In my book entitled *Is John 3:16 the gospel?* I have explained that John 3:16 is the most mistranslated, misinterpreted, misunderstood and misapplied verse in the New Testament. When you study it carefully, you find that it does not mean what we thought it meant. I must simply allude to some of the key points here which I have examined more fully elsewhere. That verse was never intended to be the gospel, but we have made it the gospel, and we quote it more than any other verse. Above all, we quote it out of context, and when you treat a verse in that way you invariably get the wrong meaning. I am sure that you can tell me what John 3:16 says without looking in your Bible, but could you tell me what John 3:17 says? Could you tell me what John 3:15 says? Most cannot do so. Do you see what I mean? If you take a verse out of context you will not understand it. It belongs in there, and the verses around it explain what it means.

Let us take the word 'loved'. Have you ever noticed that this word ends with the letter 'd', not with the letter 's'? It does not say, 'God loves the world', it says he *loved* —and that is a past tense verb. Find someone who knows Greek and check this. The word 'loved' is in the Greek tense that means to do something once, and **once only**. Therefore, the word 'loved' in John 3:16 means that God, on one occasion, loved the world. That is a bit of a shock. And on that *one* occasion he gave – and that is in the same tense – once he gave his only begotten Son. So God loved the world once, and once gave his only Son. But the real key to that verse is the little word *so* which is in the wrong place. I am sorry to have to tell you that; in the English it is after the word 'God', and do you know how we read it? 'For God so-o-o-o loved the world', but in fact that is not the word, and it does not mean 'so much' or 'so deeply', or any of the meanings we give it. The little word 'so' comes before the word 'God' in the Greek, and should do so in the English. *For so God loved once the world.* So, just so, even so — that is what it means, it is the word *houtos*, which means *thus, in this way.* So, *for in this way, God once loved the world and once gave his only Son.*

In what way? Well, verse 16 does not tell you, but verse 15 and verse 14 tell you all about it. For in this way, for just so, for even so, God loved the world. So we go back to the previous verse. What happens in that verse? It is a reference to Numbers chapter 21, where God killed hundreds, even thousands of his own people, the Israelites, because they grumbled about the food he provided for them. Now fancy that in the verse in front of God loving the world! Extraordinary, isn't it?

You should know the story. God fed the children of Israel with the same food every day for forty years. It was there to be picked up from the desert; they had to cook it, but it kept them going. It had all the minerals, all the vitamins, all the carbohydrates and protein they needed in order to survive for forty years. They called it 'manna', which is Hebrew for 'what is it?' The children would say to the parents: not 'what-is-it' again! The people began to grumble and complain — the food in Egypt, even when we were slaves, was better than this; we had leeks and garlic, spices and curries, and now we are eating 'what is it' every day. They grumbled, so God – the same God who loved the world in verse 16 – in verse 14 sent snakes among them, and the snakes bit them and they died of poison — and God did that to punish them.

So many died that they asked Moses to go and pray to God for them. They realised they had sinned, that they should never have complained about the food. They wanted Moses to tell God they were sorry and to ask him to take the snakes away. So that is what Moses did. He went to God and told him the people were sorry. They realised it was not a coincidence that he had sent the snakes.

God told them that he was not going to take the

snakes away, but he would give them a cure for snake bite. They were to put a metal snake up on a pole on the nearest hill, and if any Israelite was bitten by a snake, all they had to do would be to go to that pole and gaze on the snake, a bronze snake hanging on the pole, and if they looked they would be cured. He was not going to take the death threat away – they deserved that, and it was going to stay – but he was offering them a cure.

Jesus said, *'As Moses lifted up the serpent in the wilderness, even so'* [and there is the same word, just *so*] *'the Son of Man will be lifted up.'* Then it goes straight on: *'for just so, for in the same way, God gave his only Son.'*

You see, the whole human race is under a threat of death because of our treatment of God. And God has not taken away that threat, he has given us an antidote, and the antidote is Jesus on the cross. Do you understand that? That is the context of John 3:16 — a God who kills people for grumbling about the food he has given them: same God, same love that provides an antidote.

Let us return to the word *love*. I am sure you

will have heard from preachers about this. The Greek language is much richer than the English language. We use the word 'love' for a whole lot of things. We just have one word 'love' for all the different kinds of love, for which the Greeks had at least four words: the love of addiction – what we tend to call 'lust' – had one word; the love of attraction – mainly sexual attraction between men and women – had another word, *eros*; the love of friendship, the love of affection had yet another word, *philio* (and Philadelphia means brotherly love), but none of those words was used of God. They had to find a new word – *agape* – a relatively rare word in the Greek language. (Incidentally, the statue in Piccadilly Circus is not *eros* but *agape*, and it is a memorial to Lord Shaftesbury, Anthony Ashley Cooper, for his work in getting children out of coal mines and of limiting working hours in factories. And it was put up as a statue of the angel of mercy; it is not Cupid at all — do not believe that rubbish! There is a lot of 'eros' that goes on around Piccadilly Circus, but that statue is not *eros*, it is *agape*.)

'*Agape*' is always an active word. You do not *feel* it, you *do* it. Here is the difference between *agape* and even the highest human love: you do it to people you do not like, to people who are your enemies, to people who hate you. It is comparatively easy to 'do' love to those you like, or who like you. *'Greater love has no-one than this, that he lay down his life for his friends'* [NIV] — that is the highest love among human beings, and God's love goes way beyond that: while we were his enemies Christ died for us — that is *agape*. When a man said to Jesus, *'How do I agape my neighbour?'* Jesus told the parable of the good Samaritan. The secret of that parable is that Samaritans and Jews hated each other. You will never understand why the hero is a Samaritan unless you know that. The Jew was walking down the road to Jericho — to go seventy miles out of his way to go to Galilee, to avoid meeting any Samaritans. Now you discover the meaning of the story. When the Samaritan saw the Jew, his enemy from a hated ethnic group, helpless and in need, he was the only one who went and did something for him. That is *agape*.

It reaches out to the unlovely, to the ungrateful, to the hateful, to the horrible. And when men are helpless and in desperate need, then *agape* is a reaction to that situation which transforms itself into action. That is the sort of love God has, and that is why every mention of his love is linked to the cross. *God demonstrates his own love for us in this: While we were still sinners, Christ died for us.* [NIV] If you just tell unbelievers 'God loves you' they will assume very quickly that they must be likeable, loveable, attractive to God. They will not realise that it is precisely because they are unlovely to God – because he hates how they live and what they do – that it becomes so marvellous that he sent his Son to die for them. And perhaps that is why the love of God is only spoken of in the Bible to the redeemed. They are the only ones who will appreciate it; they are the only ones who understand how much God hated what they were doing and what they were, and then to know that he has forgiven them. You see, love and forgiveness belong together. A certain woman once came to Jesus and they said, 'Doesn't he know what kind of a woman that is? She is a woman of the streets.' And Jesus said, 'She loves me so much because she has been forgiven so much.' Only the forgiven understand what God's love is like. Therefore I am convinced we should keep that 'pearl' away from those who will misunderstand it, jump to wrong conclusions and put together a wrong concept of God.

I believe that this concept of God as love, and nothing but love, is actually driving people away from church. A report on why churches are emptying was carried out by an 'Ecumenical Research Committee', comprising different denominations. They questioned 14,000 people, asking, 'Why have you stopped going to church? Why don't you go to church regularly?' The report was entitled 'Church Survey – help your church grow', but in fact the advertisement for it read 'Why are many churches empty? Discover the answer.' They found that all the answers that were given by ordinary people in the street (and there were only five answers specified in the whole report) were astonishing, for one of the main reasons given was that there was too much 'love talk'; that they had been told God loves you anyway; God loves you just as you are; God's love is unconditional. Far from producing respect for God, far from producing the fear of the Lord that is the beginning of wisdom, it had the opposite effect: a God who loses respect.

Many of these people who had voted with their feet were saying, 'Why don't we hear more about the holiness of God and the righteousness of God?' I was astonished to hear things like that said by people who had left church, but they were saying all this 'lovey dovey' talk has reduced even our worship to a kind of 'pally-ness'. One man said to me: 'In our church we worship God all-matey.' I thought, you have put your finger right on it!

Where is that fear, that awe and reverence; that awareness that we worship God who is a raging fire? I have only ever twice been anywhere near a raging fire. Once was in Australia, a bush fire. We were fleeing in a car through the smoke, and the flames were travelling at sixty miles an hour, because eucalyptus trees are full of inflammable oil, and you had to drive along county roads at seventy or eighty miles an hour to escape from that raging fire! I can tell you, I had funny feelings in the pit of my stomach, and I thought, 'Why do I never have those feelings in church?' The New Testament says *Let us worship God with awe and reverence, for our God is a raging fire.*

The other time was when I was flying home from Sicily. The pilot said, 'I'll give you a treat. Mount Etna is erupting, and I'll fly you right over it so you can see it!' I was on the left-hand side of the plane, the port side, and he literally flew over the mouth of the volcano. We could see the boiling lava below, and the lava destroying houses on the hillside. He tipped the plane right up and flew in a tight circle until I was looking straight down. As I knew a bit about the airflow that can happen over a volcano I was praying that he would move on quickly, and finally, to my relief, he straightened up and flew to Heathrow. Why don't I ever feel like that in church? The Bible says that this is how we should feel in the presence of Almighty God. But it is not always like that today, is it?

We begin now to see the difficulty of talking

about God's love to an unbelieving world. That ecumenical report quoted some things the people said, and one quote was: 'God loves you, no matter what you do.' That is a straight lie. My Bible does not talk about an unconditional love, it says things like this: *God loves those who fear him*; *God loves those who keep his commands*. That does not sound 'unconditional' to me. Some have tried to say that the real contrast in God is between the God of the Old Testament and the God of the New. Have you heard that one? It goes back to a man called Marcion in the fifth century, and the heresy is called Marcionism, after him. It is the heresy that the God of the Old Testament is harsh, cruel, unkind, and the God of the New Testament is loving, compassionate, kind. It is a very common impression on the part of those who do not know their Bibles well enough, and I am sad to say that there are evangelical communicators in the media who have revived that heresy and criticised the 'God of the Old Testament'. How can you say that the 'love of God' curses people? It is a nonsense. How can you say the 'love of God' kills people? It is a nonsense. It is not love that binds the two sides of his character together, it is something else, and I want to explore that now. **It is his sheer goodness**. **So should we not actually be talking to the world about the goodness of God?**

I was asked to take an evangelistic series of meetings in a town hall in Gloucestershire and in a university in New Zealand. I was asked, 'Could you give us a title for your talks?'

I said, very simply, two words: 'Good God'. Then I continued, 'That sums up everything I believe about God.' To my horror, in both places, they put out huge posters with a dreadful photograph of me, making me look like a monster, like Dracula, and then above it were the words 'GOOD GOD!' Well, I can tell you that the venues were packed on the first nights! 'Good God' is a pair of words which many use as an expletive when they hit the wrong nail with the hammer, or when they are surprised. People do not know what they are saying. God *is* good. That is the word that comes from Genesis chapter 1. Everything he did was good because he is good.

But the word 'good' has been devalued and has lost its meaning. Like the word 'love' it will be misunderstood. We use the word 'good' in so many different ways. 'Just had a good meal'; 'have you had a good holiday?'; 'hope the weather will be good tomorrow'; and we even talk about a good dog and use the same word for God — extraordinary! What do we mean by 'good'? We have relativised it to the point that it is no longer an absolute word. It should mean 'absolutely perfect', but we never use it like that; we use it of anyone or anything that gives us pleasure or decreases pain. 'He's a good dentist.' Do you mean he is highly skilled, or do you mean he can do the work painlessly? Anything that gives us pleasure is called 'good'.

One day, a man came to Jesus and said, *'Good master, what must I do to inherit eternal life?'* Jesus replied, *'Why do you call me good? There is only one person who is good and that is God.'*

The word 'good' has so lost its meaning that even when we use it of God we are just being cheeky. What we mean by a good God is a God who is absolutely perfect. That is the real meaning of the word.

So we will have to find another word. Is there a word in the dictionary which is hardly ever used in normal speech but which we could use about God, that begins to convey what he is really like? There is, and I want to give it to you — the word is *righteous*. **God is righteous**. And that is what we need to be telling the world, for that is what the world most needs to hear, even if it does not want to hear it.

When Jesus prayed, he never prayed, 'Loving Father' — we do, but he never did. If you read Jesus' prayer in John 17, you find that he used two adjectives: *holy* Father and, later in the prayer, *righteous* Father. That qualifies his Fatherhood very seriously — 'righteous Father'. So what do we mean by the word 'righteous'? The negative side of righteousness is that God can never do anything wrong. I once got a sheet of paper and wrote at the top of it: 'Things Almighty God cannot do.' Within five minutes I had written thirty things Almighty God cannot do. The first things I wrote were: he cannot tell a lie; he cannot have an impure thought; he cannot break a promise. After writing thirty things down, I realised with a shock that I had done all of them, and that did not make me feel that I am greater than Almighty God, it made me feel very much smaller. There are many things God cannot do. Thank God he is righteous. He has no favourites; he cannot be bribed; you cannot bargain with God; you cannot corrupt him in any way; his judgement of every one of us will be absolutely fair because he knows the whole truth.

Incidentally, that is why I entitled my auto-biography *Not as Bad as the Truth*. Years ago, some naughty people in Wales began to spread some rumours about me which were totally untrue, and they hurt. Not only that, but they began to close doors of ministry. When people heard these lies they wrote to me and said, 'We are very sorry but arrangements for your visit have fallen through.'

I went to God and complained about this. I said, 'God, it is painful. They are telling lies and it is closing doors for ministry.'

Then the Lord spoke to me as clearly as when I speak out loud myself: 'David, the worst they can say about you is not as bad as the truth.' And I burst out laughing with relief because they did not know the worst! When I told my wife she roared with laughter because she knows the worst. So that is how the book gained its title.

But the Lord then added, 'I know the worst, but I still love you and use you,' and that could be said of everyone who does his work. God is absolutely fair, absolutely just, with no favourites. You will never be able to accuse God of injustice. That is the negative side. On the positive side, everything he does is absolutely right. Abraham argued with him about this. 'Will you destroy Sodom if there are forty good people in it?'

'No.'

'Twenty?' It came right down —five! And it was Abraham who said to God, *'Shall not the judge of the earth be right?'* The God who runs our whole universe cannot do anything wrong and will always do what is right. As a pastor I was often asked by couples who had lost a baby, 'What has happened to our baby? Has it gone to heaven? Where is it?' I would say, 'I don't know, the Bible does not give the answer to that question.' But I also used to say this: 'If you knew God as well as I know him, you would know that whatever he has done with your baby is absolutely right. I do not have all the answers to all the questions, the Bible does not, but it tells us that whatever God does – with our babies or with us – will be absolutely right.' What security and comfort that gives us, to be in a world run by the one who always does what is right.

Therefore we can add two more things which the Bible adds. The first is that one day he will punish all evil. When I read about teenagers breaking into pensioners' flats in London, and raping old ladies and getting away with it as far as the police are concerned (the majority of crimes are not discovered), I comfort myself with the thought that one day God will deal with those young men. Nobody will get away with anything, because God is righteous. If the world believed this, then you would see crime figures coming down dramatically, but crime is increasing because criminals think they can get away with it. However, they will not get away with their actions — every single act is recorded in heaven, and one day books will be opened.

The second thing God has promised to do is not only to punish all evil but also to banish all evil, and have a world in which there is nothing evil. He is determined to have that. It is why he made this world, but he is going to make another one. There will be a new heaven and a new earth wherein righteousness dwells, and we are told about that new heaven and new earth. I am looking forward to being in a world where everything is right and nothing is wrong.

THE GOSPEL OF RIGHTEOUSNESS

But the only people who will ever get in to that new world are righteous people, and when I say 'righteous' I mean perfect people, people who never do things that are wrong, always do things that are right. We do not stand a chance of getting in, do we? Sometimes people say to me – and I cannot help laughing – 'Why doesn't God get rid of all the wicked people in the world now? Then the rest of us could live in peace and happiness!' There is a flaw in that argument somewhere! It is amazing how many people think that it is everybody else spoiling the world, not them. An opinion poll found that 70% of the people in the USA believe they are going to heaven, and 70% of the people in America believed they knew someone who was going to hell! Once again, the statistics do not add up! So really, what I have written so far damns you. If the new heaven and the new earth are only for righteous people, for perfect people, none of us has a chance of ever making it, however hard we try. And when you try to be righteous you finish up worse than you began, because you begin to be proud that you are righteous, you begin to feel you are better than other people (*I thank you that I am not as other men are*), and you cannot be proud of your own goodness without despising people who are not so good. Pride and contempt are two sides of the same coin.

So is there hope? Yes. There is a gospel, there is good news, but what is that gospel? Or to put it this way: what is the offer of the gospel? What does Christianity offer people that cannot be found anywhere else? You would be amazed how many different answers people give. 'Well, it gives you a purpose in life'; 'It gives you peace in your mind'; 'It gives you a clear conscience'; 'It keeps you healthy, wealthy'; and, very commonly, 'It saves you from going to hell'—as if the gospel is a fire escape!   None of those is the answer of the New Testament. They are all by-products of the gospel. Somebody who responds to the gospel is likely to find a purpose and a peace. That is not the offer of the gospel. What is the offer of the gospel? It is not an offer of a God who loves you. Neither Jesus nor the apostles ever preached a gospel of God's love — check me out. So what does the gospel offer? Here are some words from the apostle Paul:

I am not ashamed of the gospel, for it is the power of God for salvation to everyone who goes on believing, first to the Jew and then to the Gentile. For in it is revealed a righteousness from God, a righteousness which is by faith from beginning to end, even as it is written, 'the righteous shall live by faith'.

There is not a word about God's love there, but three times an offer of righteousness — not the righteousness *of* God, but a righteousness *from* God. We will never make it, we will never be righteous enough to live in a righteous new heaven and new earth, but God is offering us his righteousness. He is saying you will never have enough of your own, try having mine. That is an amazing offer, is it not?

He does it in two stages, two phases. Stage one is **imputed righteousness** and stage two is **imparted righteousness**. In the first stage he treats you as if you are already righteous and calls you a saint. We call it **justification by faith**. And having done that and restored a relationship with himself, he then imparts his righteousness to you. He does the first through Christ and the second through the Holy Spirit. That is why to be saved we need both the second and third persons of the Trinity; some people think we only need Christ to be saved, but no, if you want to finish up in a righteous universe you need the Holy Spirit as well as Jesus Christ. The first (imputed righteousness) amounts to forgiveness, God wiping out your past. If God forgave sin without any conditions it would be unrighteous of him. It would be immoral for a righteous God to overlook sin in my life; he would be fooling himself, never mind us, in saying you are a saint now, you are a holy person now, and yet that is what he does. However, there is no such thing as *unconditional* forgiveness. Again, that adjective would be totally misplaced. It would be wrong for a good and righteous God to forgive sin, unless two conditions were met. Number one, that those sins had been paid for already. This is the heart of the gospel: that Jesus has paid. That is why there can be no forgiveness without the cross; that is why every act of forgiveness is written in the blood of Jesus; that is what your forgiveness cost, and that is why we have bread and wine regularly, to remind us of what it cost.

But there is another condition. That was a condition that God had to meet, and he has met it. *Thus, just so, God loved the world that he once gave his only Son.* That is the cost. But the other condition is on our side, and it is that we **repent**. It would be absolutely immoral if God forgave us without our repentance, and repentance is something you do, it is a change of lifestyle. Now repentance has all but disappeared, because if you just talk about God's love and say 'all you need to do is accept God's love for you', then repentance goes out of the window, and yet this was the very first thing that John the Baptist told people to do, that Jesus told people to do, that Peter told people to do, and that Paul told people to do. I am sure you know the passage where Paul said, *I was not disobedient to the heavenly vision*, but can you complete it? I am afraid I find that very few Christians can, and I have never heard a preacher preach on what follows. Paul goes on to say: *I was not disobedient to the heavenly vision . . . I preached repentance to the Gentiles that they should turn to God and prove their repentance by their deeds.*

Why have I never heard that preached? Because we are not called on these days to repent first. It means you cannot come to God as you are, you must first change. Repentance is 'being sorry enough to stop'!

Let me tell you two stories. First, I was preaching at a theatre in Scotland for three nights of evangelism, and on the second night a young woman came up to me at the end. She was shaking, she was crying, her face was blotchy — she was upset. And she said, 'Mr Pawson, you frustrate me.'

I replied, 'How have I frustrated you?'

'You have made me want to be a Christian.'

I said to her, 'That's why I came to Aberdeen; what's frustrating about that?'

She answered, 'I have tried to be a Christian for eighteen months; I have gone forward at every evangelistic meeting. I have been counselled; I have been through classes. Nothing has happened, nothing has changed, and I had come to the conclusion there is nothing in this Christianity. A friend brought me here tonight and you have made me want it all over again.' She continued, 'I have tried and it doesn't work.'

I looked her in the eye and asked, 'Who are you living with?'

She said, 'A young man.'

Then I asked, 'Are you married to him?'

'No.'

'Are you living as if you were married?'

'Yes.'

'Why aren't you married?'

'Well, he doesn't believe in marriage; he says, as long as we love each other that is all that matters.'

'Well,' I replied, 'if he leaves you tomorrow he will not have broken any promises, because he hasn't made any.'

She said, 'He won't leave me tomorrow, he loves me too much.'

I said, 'Well, I'm very sorry but you have got a very difficult decision to make, and I can't make it for you. You have to decide which man you want to live with, your young man or Jesus, but you can't live with both.'

Then she got really angry with me. She said, 'No-one else told me that.'

I said, 'But no-one else has been able to help you and I'm trying to help you.'

I would love to tell you that she was converted on the spot, but she wasn't, she ran out of that theatre sobbing her heart out, and I felt exactly how Jesus felt when the rich young ruler went away sad. Jesus had given him a choice: it is your money or me.

It is called repentance; very few preachers and evangelists are preaching for repentance today.

The other story is of Paul, a young man who had

a big motorbike with huge handlebars and mirrors sticking out like a porcupine – you know the kind of thing. He rode up to my front door once and rang the bell, and I said, 'What is it Paul?'

He said, 'I want to talk.' He was wearing a leather jacket, covered with brass studs. He came into our house then squirmed his way into our settee, which bore the marks forever after that!

I said, 'What do you want to talk about, Paul?'

He said, 'I want to be baptised.'

I asked, 'Do you know how we baptise people here?'

'Yeah, you duck 'em in the water,' he answered.

I replied, 'So you want me to duck you in the water?'

'Yeah.'

'Paul,' I said, 'do you know the meaning of the word "repent"?'

'No.'

I said, 'Well, go home and ask Jesus this question: is there anything in my life you don't like, Jesus? Cut it out and come back.'

Three weeks later I heard that motorbike, and

there was Paul on the doorstep. I said, 'Well, what is it, Paul?'

He held out his hands and said, 'There.'

I said, 'What do you mean?'

'There.'

I asked again, 'What is it?'

He said to me, 'I've stopped biting my nails.'

Now you may laugh at that, but he was producing more evidence of repentance than many people who get baptised — and he meant it. He was proving to me exactly what Paul said, proving his repentance by his deeds, and so we baptised him and he never looked back.

Repentance is the very first step into the kingdom – the very first step in becoming a Christian – and it means turning your back on the way you live. It means a change of lifestyle; it may mean getting out of a wrong relationship; it may mean so many different things, and the Holy Spirit will tell you what it means. But you see, just telling people God loves them does not lead to that. Telling them God is righteous and will one day deal with all evil in our world — that does.

The gospel is an offer — but not just of forgiveness, for that is only a beginning. It is an offer of righteousness; it is an offer of making bad people into good people, sinners into saints.

I was invited to preach in the Temple in the Strand, to a gathering of the judges, barristers and solicitors of London. The pulpit was like a dock and, looking down on them all, it appeared to me as though they were wearing wigs — they were not, but it looked like that. Lord Denning read the lesson. Standing in the dock, I thought I would try to be a bit humorous. Fatal! The Temple is a round building and the acoustics are dreadful; you hear yourself five or six times. So I began by saying, 'I have been told the agnostics in this building are dreadful!' Nobody smiled! Afterwards somebody took me aside and told me that it was Lord Denning's favourite joke. So it fell flat.

So what did I preach on? I preached from Romans chapter 8, where Paul says, *What the law could not do . . . God did.* I said to all those lawyers, 'I'm going to talk about something you can't do.' Cheeky, wasn't it? But I continued, 'You can punish the wrongdoer, you can even discourage other wrongdoers by your punishment, but the one thing you cannot do is to make a bad man into a good man — that is what the gospel does.'

I have preached in top security jails in Britain, to murderers and drug pushers in for life. And I could take you to one prison where an entire wing has been utterly transformed by the gospel of righteousness. These once bad men are now good men. The walls of the cells were knocked down so that they could live as a brotherhood, and the officers who used to come into that wing three at a time for safety could come in one at a time and knock on the cell door, and the prisoners would say, 'Come in, make your coffee, and we will read a bit of the Bible to you.'

The governor could hardly believe what has happened to all the men in that wing — an entire wing of good men! That is the power of the gospel.

We need to be aware that unrighteousness is no problem to God. If a man will repent of his unrighteousness, God can do wonders. He will treat him as a saint from then on, and he will make him into a saint. Do you realise that the cross was a double substitution? It is only preached, in many ways, as a single substitution — that he became sin for us, and that he was our substitute and was punished for what we had done. But it was a double substitution. Listen to the Bible: *God made him who had no sin to be sin for us, so that in him we might become the righteousness of God.* [NIV]

It is a double exchange: **give him your sins and take his righteousness**. It is not a fair exchange, but it is a good one. So many people want Jesus to take their sins away, but they do not want to take his righteousness. They want to hang on to their bad habits; they want to hang on to those besetting sins which dog their footsteps; they want to keep a little bit of unrighteousness.

Did you ever read the *Just William* books by Richmal Crompton? Have you read the one where William gets converted? Somebody comes to preach at the Sunday school he attends and he decides he is going to be a Christian. He thinks it is high time he turned over a new leaf, from all his mischief and from all the tricks that he has played. So he decides that he will do that on the Tuesday, and spend the Monday doing all the bad things he has always longed to do, because, after all, he is going to be a saint on the Tuesday! And on the Monday he paints the cat green, smashes all the windows in the greenhouse and does everything he has always longed to do. He comes home at night thinking: it is going to be wonderful, tomorrow. He was going to be a saint, a good boy for the rest of his life. Just as he is falling off to sleep, he remembers that there was one thing he had intended to do that he had forgotten to do, and then he remembers another thing to do — and you can guess the rest of the story, he never really gets converted, because he never really repents. Well, unrighteousness is no problem to God **provided there is true repentance**.

But the thing that God can do nothing about is something that is rife inside the church, as well as outside, and that is self-righteousness. God can do nothing with self-righteous people who think they are good, who think they are better than other people, but who are nowhere near God's standards. They do not realise it because they are always measuring themselves by others, by the people next door and the people down the road. And as long as you compare yourself with other people you will think you are righteous, and it is **self-righteousness**. I was having my hair cut and I thought it was time I talked to the hairdresser. As he was cutting my hair, he said, out of the blue, 'I'm as good as any who go to your church.'

I said, 'I don't think you can say that until you know them better; you might be right, but that's not going to help you.'

He said, 'Why not?'

I replied, 'Are you as good as Jesus?'

The conversation stopped and he went silent, then he said, 'Well, perhaps not quite.' It was the beginning of seeing himself as he really was. He was a self-righteous man because he thought he was good by comparing himself with others. That is what an awful lot of people are doing.

I once went to speak at a Baptist Women's League. That is not my scene, and I felt like a lion in a den of Daniels! But I went. A large lady who was the chairperson, in a fur coat I think, came to me and said, 'What are you going to speak about?'

'Grace,' I replied.

'Oh,' she said, 'that sounds nice.'

So I got up before all those women (some of whom were knitting) and said, 'I want to say just two things about grace. Number one: your bad deeds need not keep you out of heaven.' Oh they liked that, they really responded, smiling. Then I said, 'The second thing about grace is that your good deeds won't help you to get there.' Their faces fell. The chairperson came to me afterwards, bristling with indignation. She said, 'Are you telling me all the good things I have done have been wasted?'

I said, 'No, they weren't wasted for other people, but they won't help you.' One of the most difficult parts of repentance is to repent of your good deeds – it is much harder than repenting of your bad deeds – to repent of your self-righteousness, which is far more offensive to God than your unrighteousness.

The Bible says some pretty blunt things, crude things, about self-righteousness. I give you just two of them. Forgive the language, but it is in the original Hebrew and Greek. Isaiah says our righteousness is like a used menstrual cloth to God. That is not something you are proud to display or boast about to others, and that is what Isaiah said to the women of Jerusalem. And Paul claimed to be a righteous man — a self-righteous man, a Pharisee who kept all the commandments. He reckoned his legalistic 'righteousness' *shit* that he might gain Christ. He used a crude Greek word which is exactly equivalent to that. Our Bibles say 'dung', or even 'rubbish' (NIV) but it is nothing of the kind. His teaching means that if you are self-righteous it is like a little boy going to God with a potty full of his own dirt and saying, 'Look what I have done.' It is as disgusting to God as that. Self-righteousness is keeping more people out of the kingdom than any unrighteousness, because it is so difficult to repent of it, so difficult to admit that you need his forgiveness.

I believe we are damaging our cause by throwing

'pearls' to 'pigs', by talking about 'God loves you' to people who have never been redeemed or forgiven. I was astonished to read that report saying that is one of the five things that is losing respect for the church. But of course, if you say, 'God loves you whatever you do', then why bother? Why repent? Why go to church? Why read your Bible? Why even try to be righteous? If God loves me unconditionally, it is okay. The thought becomes: 'He would never send me to hell because his love is unconditional!' I believe we are doing ourselves a great disservice. Let us return to Jesus and the apostles. They preached **a gospel of righteousness**. They preached God's wrath as well as his love. Paul, in Romans chapter 1, went straight on to talk about the wrath of God, which was the beginning of his judgement — and the wrath of God is on this country as clearly as anything you can see. Let us tell them what God is really like: that he is absolutely righteous, absolutely good, can never do anything wrong, and will one day punish and banish all evil from the universe. That is good news.

PRAYER

Righteous Father, thank you for showing us what you are really like. Thank you that no-one can change you, no-one can influence you; you are God; you are above us, greater than any of us. We pray that you will give us such an understanding of yourself, such knowledge of you as you really are, that we may reach out to our communities, that we will be able to communicate the truth. May we show them your love, and may we tell them about your righteousness. Thank you that you can make bad people into good people, sinners into saints, and that is the good news. So to you be the glory, the praise and the honour, for ever and ever. *Amen.*